# Snacks & Desserts

# Snacks & Desserts

*Chefs' Special*

Compiled by
Master Chefs
of India

**Lustre Press**
**Roli Books**

# Gourmet Delight

In a land so rich in cultural heritage, it is but natural that the Indian cuisine is multifarious, offering a delight to both the eye and the palate. Its myriad flavours and cooking traditions find their roots in its historical influences. The Mughals revolutionised the art of Indian cooking with their delectable *biryanis* (an exquisite oven preparation with meat/vegetables, herbs and seasonings), *kormas* (a spicy meat or vegetarian preparation), *kebabs* and *tikkas* (meat and vegetables cooked in small pieces, usually on skewers) made in a *tandoor* (an oven made of mud and heated by a slow charcoal fire). The British Raj spawned an interesting Anglo-Indian gastronomic culture which is still eaten with relish. Different regions in India offer their own specialities with their very own taste, subtlety and aroma. The country's vast reservoir of spices made from its abundance of tropical herbs, serves as garnishing and contains medicinal and preservative properties. Indeed the range of the Indian cuisine can amaze even a connoisseur.

This book offers a treat of mouth-watering *Snacks & Desserts* for vegetarians and non-vegetarians. Soul-warming soups, a luscious assortment of snacks and all-time favourite desserts, can together substitute for an entire meal. A few basic recipes of popular cooking ingredients, Indian equivalents of foods given in each list of ingredients and a Glossary of Cooking Terms are valuable add-ons. Multi-purpose chutneys serve as a complementary fillip. And to provide a finishing touch, a sprinkling of 'handy hints' are added as sure-fire remedies to common culinary problems.

# BASIC INDIAN RECIPES

**Green Chilli Paste**
Chop the required quantity of green chillies and process until pulped.

**Garam Masala (for 450 gm)**
Put 200 gm cumin, 35 gm peppercorns, 45 gm black cardamoms, 30 gm green cardamoms, 60 gm coriander seeds, 20 gm cloves, 20 gm cinnamon sticks, 15 gm bayleaves and 2 nutmegs in a processor and grind to a fine powder. Transfer to a bowl, add 20 gm mace powder and 30 gm ginger powder and mix well. Sieve and store in an airtight container.

**Brown Onion Paste**
Fry sliced onions over medium heat till brown. Drain excess oil and allow to cool. Process until pulped, (using very little water, if required). Refrigerate in an airtight container.

**Yoghurt**
Boil milk and keep aside till lukewarm. Add 2 tsp yoghurt to the milk and mix well. Allow to ferment for 6-8 hours.

**Red Chilli Paste**
Chop red chillies and process until pulped.

### Ginger/Garlic Paste
Soak ginger/garlic overnight. Peel, chop and process to pulp. Refrigerate in an airtight container.

### Onion Paste
Peel and quarter onions and process until pulped. Refrigerate in an airtight container.

### Tomato Purée
Peel, deseed and chop the tomatoes. Transfer to a pan, add 1 lt water, 8 cloves, 8 green cardamoms, 15 gm ginger, 10 gm garlic, 5 bayleaves and 5 peppercorns and cook on medium heat till the tomatoes are tender. Cool and process to a pulp.

### Cottage Cheese (*Paneer*)
Heat 3 lt milk. Just before it boils, add 60 ml/4 tsp lemon juice or white ginger. Strain the milk through a muslin cloth and hang for 2-3 hours to drain the whey and moisture.

### Khoya
Boil milk in a wok (*kadhai*). Reduce heat and cook, stirring occasionally, till the quantity is reduced to half. Then stir constantly and scrape from all sides till a thick paste-like consistency is obtained. Allow to cool. *Khoya* is also called wholemilk fudge.

# JHINGA NISHA

*(Exotic prawns flavoured with sesame seeds and fenugreek)*

*Serves: 4   Preparation time: 1 hour 30 minutes   Cooking time: 20 minutes*

## Ingredients

Large prawns *(bare jhinge)* 8
Lemon juice *5 ml / 1 tsp*
Ginger-garlic *(adrak-lasan)* paste (p. 8) *20 gm / 4 tsp*
Salt to taste
Sesame seeds *(til) 15 gm / 3 tsp*
Yoghurt *(dahi)* (p. 6) *20 gm / 4 tsp*
Cheddar cheese *15 gm / 3 tsp*
Cinnamon *(dalchini)* powder *5 gm / 1 tsp*
Dry fenugreek *(kasoori methi) 5 gm / 1 tsp*
White pepper *(safed mirch)* powder *5 gm / 1 tsp*
Green chillies 6
Clove *(laung)* powder *5 gm / 1 tsp*
Chaat masala *5 gm / 1 tsp*

## Method

**1.** Rub some lemon juice, the ginger-garlic paste and salt on the prawns and keep aside for half an hour.
**2.** Roast the sesame seeds and crush to a powder.
**3.** Beat the yoghurt in a bowl and add the remaining ingredients (except chaat masala and lemon juice).
**4.** Rub this mixture on the prawns and keep in a cool place for 1 hour. Preheat the oven to 150 °C / 300 °F.
**5.** Skewer the prawns and roast till light golden in colour. Apply the sesame seed powder over the prawns and roast again for 2 minutes. Sprinkle with chaat masala and lemon juice.

# GINGER LAMB CHOPS

*Serves: 4   Preparation time: 4 hours 30 minutes   Cooking time: 20 minutes*

## Ingredients

Lamb chops *12*
Papaya *(papita)* paste *30 gm / 2 tbsp*
Salt to taste
Ginger paste (p. 8) *45 gm / 3 tbsp*
Garlic paste (p. 8) *20 gm / 4 tsp*
Black pepper *(kali mirch)* powder *5 gm / 1 tsp*
Cream *45 gm / 3 tbsp*
Cumin *(jeera)* powder *15 gm / 1 tbsp*
Red chilli powder *10 gm / 2 tsp*
Garam masala (p. 6) *10 gm / 2 tsp*
Lemon juice *30 ml / 2 tbsp*
Butter / oil for basting

## Method

**1.** Clean chops and flatten them slightly with a spatula. Mix together the papaya paste, salt, ginger-garlic pastes and pepper and rub the mixture onto the chops. Keep aside for 3-4 hours.

**2.** Whisk cream along with cumin powder, red chilli powder, garam masala and lemon juice. Coat the chops well and leave to marinate further for an hour.

**3.** Preheat oven to 175 °C / 350 °F. Skewer chops an inch apart and roast in oven/tandoor/grill for 10-12 minutes.

**4.** Hang skewers for a couple of minutes to let excess liquid drip off. Baste with butter and roast again for 3-4 minutes until lightly browned. Garnish with chopped coriander and serve hot.

# BARBECUED LAMB CUBES

*Serves: 4-5   Preparation time: 6-7 hours   Cooking time: 10 minutes*

## Ingredients

Lamb (leg piece, chopped into boneless pieces) *1 kg*
Yoghurt *(dahi)* (p. 6) *150 ml / ¾ cup*
Coriander *(dhaniya)* powder *10 gm / 2 tsp*
Turmeric *(haldi)* powder *10 gm / 2 tsp*
Red chilli powder *3 gm / ½ tsp*
Ginger *(adrak)* paste (p. 8) *25 gm / 5 tsp*
Garlic *(lasan)* paste (p. 8) *25 gm / 5 tsp*
Salt to taste
Oil for basting

## Method

**1.** Mix the yoghurt, coriander powder, turmeric powder, red chilli powder, ginger and garlic pastes and salt.
**2.** Pour mixture over lamb and coat the pieces evenly.
**3.** Baste the marinated pieces with oil and cover the bowl. Chill in refrigerator for 5-6 hours, basting occasionally.
**4.** Preheat grill/tandoor/oven to 175 °C / 350 °F.
**5.** Mix meat marinade well, then skewer the pieces 2 cm apart.
**6.** Roast in grill/tandoor/oven for 5-8 minutes on each side or until cooked through, basting just once.
**7.** Serve hot, garnished with onion rings, chopped coriander and lemon wedges on a warmed serving dish. Accompany with *Anjeer ki* chutney (p. 91).

# TANDOORI BATEYR

*(Marinated and grilled quails)*

**Serves:** 4   Preparation time: 2 hours 30 minutes   Cooking time: 15 minutes

## Ingredients

Quails *(bateyr)* (100 gm each) *8*
Salt to taste
Lemon juice *60 ml / 4 tbsp*
Ginger-garlic *(adrak-lasan)* paste (p. 8) *25 gm*
Yoghurt, *(dahi)* hung (p. 6) *60 gm*
Red chilli powder *10 gm / 2 tsp*
Red chilli paste (p. 6) *30 gm*
Cumin *(jeera)* powder *15 gm / 1 tbsp*
Nutmeg *(jaiphal)* powder *5 gm / 1 tsp*
Turmeric *(haldi)* powder *5 gm / 1 tsp*
Garam masala *20 gm / 4 tsp*
Butter *60 gm*

## Method

**1.** Clean the quails and rub them with salt, lemon juice and ginger-garlic paste. Keep aside for 30 minutes.

**2.** Whisk yoghurt and add red chilli powder, red chilli paste, cumin powder, nutmeg powder, turmeric powder and garam masala. Coat the quails evenly with this mixture and keep aside for 2 hours.

**3.** Skewer the quails and roast in a moderately hot tandoor for 6-7 minutes; remove, baste with butter and roast again for 3-5 minutes.

**4.** Remove from skewers and serve hot accompanied by chutney (pp. 90-91).

# GOSHT ACHARI CHAAP

*(Lamb chops cooked with whole spices)*

*Serves: 4-5  Preparation time: 2 hours 30 minutes  Cooking time: 30 minutes*

## Ingredients

Lamb chops, on 2 bones *8 pieces*
Aniseed *(saunf) 5 gm / 1 tsp*
Black cardamoms *(bari elaichi)*
*2 gm / ½ tsp*
Black pepper *(kali mirch)*
*5 gm / 1 tsp*
Chaat masala *5 gm / 1 tsp*
Cloves *(laung) 3 gm / ²/₃ tsp*
Garlic *(lasan)* paste (p. 8)
*10 gm / 2 tsp*
Ginger *(adrak)* paste (p. 8)
*10 gm / 2 tsp*
Gram flour *(besan) 10 gm / 2 tsp*
Lemon juice *15 ml / 1 tbsp*
Mustard oil *(sarson ka tel)*
*50 ml / 3 ¹/₃ tbsp*
Mustard seeds *(rai) 5 gm / 1 tsp*
Onion seeds *(kalonji) 5 gm / 1 tsp*
Raw papaya *(kacha papita), a small piece* or meat tenderizer
Red chilli powder *15 gm / 3 tsp*
Salt to taste
Yoghurt *(dahi)* (p. 6), whisked *50 gm / ¼ cup*

## Method

**1.** Flatten the chops with a steak hammer.
**2.** Rub the chops with the papaya, ginger-garlic paste and salt; keep aside.
**3.** Roast the gram flour in a pan till light brown and sprinkle over the lamb chops.
**4.** Add the remaining ingredients to the yoghurt and

mix well to a fine batter. (Do not add chaat masala or lemon juice.)
**5.** Marinate the chops in this marinade for 2 hours.
**6.** Preheat the oven to 175 °C / 350 °F.
**7.** Skewer the chops and roast in a hot tandoor or oven until cooked.
**8.** Remove the chops from the skewers. Sprinkle with chaat masala and lemon juice and serve.

---

### *Flour for Fluff*

*For fluffy and well-shaped omelettes, add a little flour while beating the eggs.*

---

# MAANS KE SOOLEY

*(Char-broiled lamb cubes)*

*Serves: 4   Preparation time: 1 hour 30 minutes   Cooking time: 20 minutes*

## Ingredients

Lamb *1 kg*
Onions, sliced *120 gm / ½ cup*
Clarified butter (*ghee*) *120 gm / ½ cup*
Salt *10 gm / 2 tsp*
Red chilli powder *10 gm / 2 tsp*
Garlic *(lasan)* paste (p. 8) *20 gm / 4 tsp*
Raw papaya *(kacha papita)*
paste *5 gm / 1 tsp*
Charcoal pieces, live *3-4*
Cloves *(laung)* *5*
Clarified butter (*ghee*) *25 gm / 5 tbsp*

## Method

**1.** Cut the lamb into 2 ½" x 2 ½" x ¼" pieces. Clean and keep aside. Flatten each piece with a steak hammer.
**2.** Fry the sliced onions in clarified butter; drain excess clarified butter and blend to make a paste. Mix the paste with salt, red chilli powder, garlic paste and raw papaya paste and apply evenly over the pieces.
**3.** Put the lamb pieces in a bowl, leaving an open space in the centre. Place a small bowl in the centre. Put the live charcoal pieces in the bowl along with cloves and clarified butter. Cover and seal the lid. Keep aside for 1 hour.
**4.** Skewer the pieces and cook on an open spit fire till completely done. Remove and serve hot.

# CHICKEN-CHEESE SAVOURY

*Serves: 4   Preparation time: 1 hour   Cooking time: 20-30 minutes*

## Ingredients

Chicken breasts *8*
Red chilli powder *4 gm / ¾ tsp*
Garam masala (p. 6) *2 gm / ⅓ tsp*
Dry fenugreek *(kasoori methi)* powder *a pinch*
White pepper *(safed mirch)* powder *a pinch*
Salt *3 gm / ½ tsp*
Ginger-garlic *(adrak-lasan)* paste (p. 8) *15 gm / 1 tbsp*
Vinegar *(sirka) 5 ml / 1 tsp*
Oil *10 ml / 2 tsp*

**For the filling:**
Cheese, grated *600 gm / 3 cups*
Chicken tikkas chopped *200 gm / 1 cup*
Raisins *(kishmish)*, chopped *50 gm / 3 ⅓ tbsp*
Cashewnuts *(kaju)*, chopped *50 gm / 3 ⅓ tbsp*
Green coriander *(hara dhaniya)*, chopped *10 gm / 2 tsp*
Green chillies, chopped *10 gm / 2 tsp*

**For the batter:**
Cornflour *(makkai ka atta) 100 gm / ½ cup*
Water *300 ml / 1 ½ cups*
Vinegar *(sirka) 5 ml / 1 tsp*
Salt *a pinch*
White pepper *(safed mirch)* powder *a pinch*
Flour *(maida) 65 gm / 4 ⅓ tbsp*
Ginger-garlic *(adrak-lasan)* paste (p. 8) *8 gm / 1 ½ tsp*
Eggs, whisked *2*
Oil for frying

## Method

**1.** Wash, clean and dry the chicken breasts.

**2.** Mix together red chilli powder, garam masala, dry fenugreek powder, white pepper powder, salt, ginger-

garlic paste, vinegar and oil to make a paste.
**3.** Slit the chicken breasts from the sides, open out and flatten with a steak hammer, without rupturing the flesh.
**4.** Smear the chicken breasts with the prepared paste evenly.
**5. For the filling,** mix together cheese, chicken tikkas, raisins, cashewnuts, green coriander and green chillies.
**6.** Divide the filling into 8 equal portions and place in the centre of each chicken piece.
**7.** Roll the pieces firmly over the filling and refrigerate for 10 minutes.
**8. For the batter,** dissolve cornflour in water; stir well to remove any lumps. Add vinegar, salt, white pepper powder, flour, ginger-garlic paste and eggs. Mix well.
**9.** Heat oil in a wok (*kadhai*), dip each chicken piece in the cornflour batter and deep fry in medium hot oil till half done.
**10.** Remove and drain excess oil.
**11.** Just before serving, deep fry the pieces until golden brown in colour. Remove, cut into half and serve.

# TANDOORI CHAAT

*Serves: 4    Preparation time: 10 minutes    Cooking time: 10 minutes*

## Ingredients

Tandoori chicken, shredded *2*
Lemon juice *15 ml / 1 tbsp*
Salt to taste
Red chilli powder *3 gm / ½ tsp*
Oil *15 ml / 1 tbsp*
Raw green mangoes *(kacha hara aam) 100 gm / ½ cup*
Onions, finely sliced *100 gm / ½ cup*
Green chillies, chopped *10 gm / 2 tsp*
Green coriander *(hara dhaniya)*, chopped *45 gm / 3 tbsp*
Chaat masala *10 gm / 2 tsp*
Ginger *(adrak)*, chopped *5 gm / 1 tsp*

## Method

**1.** Prepare a lemon dressing by mixing together the lemon juice along with salt, red chilli powder and oil. Keep aside.
**2.** Cut the raw mango into strips.
**3.** In a mixing bowl, add the mango strips, onions, green chillies, green coriander and chaat masala, along with the shredded chicken and the lemon dressing. Mix well.
**4.** Remove to a serving bowl and serve immediately, garnished with chopped ginger.

# SHOLA KEBABS

*(Spicy, aromatic tandoori lamb cubes)*

*Serves: 4   Preparation time: 2 hours   Cooking time: 15-20 minutes*

## Ingredients

Lamb, cut into boneless pieces *900 gm*
Salt *15 gm / 1 tbsp*
Red chilli powder *8 gm / 1 tsp*
White pepper (*safed mirch*) powder *a pinch*
Fenugreek (*methi*) powder *a pinch*
Green cardamom (*choti elaichi*) powder *a pinch*
Garam masala (p. 6) *4 gm / ¾ tsp*
Onion seeds (*kalonji*), crushed *4 gm / ¾ tsp*
Fennel (*saunf*) seeds, crushed *a pinch*
Mustard (*rai*) seeds, crushed *a pinch*
Cumin (*jeera*) seeds, crushed *a pinch*
Coriander (*dhaniya*) seeds, crushed *a pinch*
Ginger-garlic (*adrak-lasan*) paste (p. 8) *35 gm / 2 ⅓ tbsp*
Raw papaya (*kacha papita*), grated *60 gm / 4 tbsp*
Mustard oil (*sarson ka tel*) *100 ml / ½ cup*
Vinegar (*sirka*) *20 ml / 4 tsp*
Yoghurt (*dahi*) (p. 6) *100 gm / ½ cup*
Butter for basting *20 gm / 4 tsp*

## Method

**1.** Wash, clean and pat dry the lamb pieces.
**2.** Mix together all the ingredients; marinate the lamb pieces in the marinade for an hour and a half.
**3.** Skewer the marinated lamb pieces and roast in a medium hot tandoor for 10-12 minutes.
**4.** Baste with butter and roast again for 5 minutes. Remove from skewers and serve hot, accompanied by chutney (pp. 90-91).

# CHUTNEYED POTATOES

*Serves: 3-4   Preparation time: 20 minutes   Cooking time: 30 minutes*

## Ingredients

Potatoes, peeled 600 gm
Mint *(pudina)*, fresh 5 gm / 1 tsp
Lemon juice 30 ml / 2 tbsp
Green chillies 3
Green coriander *(hara dhaniya)*, chopped 100 gm / ½ cup
Oil 100 ml / ½ cup
Ginger *(adrak)* paste (p. 8) 10 gm / 2 tsp
Garlic *(lasan)* paste (p. 8) 10 gm / 2 tsp
Cumin *(jeera)* powder 5 gm / 1 tsp
Coriander *(dhaniya)* powder 8 gm / 1 ½ tsp
Red chilli paste (p. 6) 8 gm / 1 ½ tsp
Salt to taste

## Method

**1.** Blend together fresh mint, lemon juice, green chillies and green coriander into a purée.

**2.** Heat oil in a heavy-bottomed pan. Add ginger-garlic pastes and potatoes. Stir-fry for 2-3 minutes. Add cumin powder, coriander powder and red chilli paste. Stir-fry, add salt and 250 ml water. Bring to a boil and simmer till the potatoes are cooked.

**3.** Add the blended purée and stir-fry for 4-5 minutes. Add salt, if necessary, and serve at once.

# COTTAGE CHEESE TIKKAS

*Serves: 4-5    Preparation time: 2 hours 15 minutes    Cooking time: 10 minutes*

## Ingredients

Cottage cheese *(paneer)* (p. 8) *1 kg*
Caraway seeds *(shahi jeera)* *3 gm / ½ tsp*
White pepper *(safed mirch)* powder *5 gm / 1 tsp*
Garam masala (p. 6) *10 gm / 2 tsp*
Turmeric *(haldi)* powder *5 gm / 1 tsp*
Lemon juice *25 ml / 5 tsp*
Salt to taste
Cream *150 ml / ¾ cup*
Yoghurt *(dahi)* (p. 6), hung *150 gm / ¾ cup*
Gram flour *(besan)* / cornflour *(makkai ka atta) 30 gm / 2 tbsp*
Fenugreek *(methi)* powder *5 gm / 1 tsp*
Garlic *(lasan)* paste (p. 8) *15 gm / 1 tbsp*
Ginger *(adrak)* paste (p. 8) *15 gm / 1 tbsp*
Red chilli powder *10 gm / 2 tsp*
Saffron *(kesar) 3 gm / ½ tsp*
Cottage cheese *(paneer)* (p. 8), grated *60 gm / 4 tbsp*
Butter to baste *50 gm / ¼ cup*
Chaat masala *10 gm / 2 tsp*

## Method

**1.** Wash and cut the paneer into small cubes (30 pieces).

**2.** Mix the caraway seeds, white pepper powder, garam masala, turmeric powder, two-thirds of the lemon juice and salt. Sprinkle over the paneer cubes. Keep aside for 1 hour in the refrigerator.

**3.** Mix cream, yoghurt and gram flour / cornflour in a bowl. Add the remaining ingredients and whisk well to make a fine batter.

**4.** Add the paneer cubes to this and marinate for at least 1 hour.
**5.** Preheat the oven to 150-175 °C / 300-350 °F).
**6.** Thread the paneer cubes onto the skewers, 2 cm apart.
**7.** Roast in an oven/tandoor/charcoal grill for 5-6 minutes. Baste with melted butter.
**8.** Sprinkle with chaat masala and the remaining lemon juice. Serve with a green salad and Sesame seed and tomato chutney (p. 90).

---

### *Lime-n-Lemony*

*Put a lemon in hot water before squeezing it.*
*You will get more juice out of it.*

---

# POMEGRANATE POTATOES

*Serves: 4-6   Preparation time: 30 minutes   Cooking time: 15-20 minutes*

## Ingredients

Potatoes, boiled, cut into 1 ½" cubes *1 kg*
Butter *100 gm / ½ cup*
Coriander *(dhaniya)* powder *15 gm / 1 tbsp*
Turmeric *(haldi)* powder *3 gm / ½ tsp*
Red chilli powder *6 gm / 1 tsp*
Pomegranate seeds *(anardana)*, dried, crushed *200 gm / 1 cup*
Salt to taste
Green chillies, slit *6*
Green coriander *(hara dhaniya)*, chopped *20 gm / 4 tsp*

## Method

**1.** Heat butter in a heavy-bottomed pan. Add coriander powder, turmeric powder, red chilli powder and half the pomegranate seeds and stir.

**2.** Mix in potatoes. Sprinkle salt and green chillies. Mix gently, so that the spices coat the potatoes evenly. Reduce heat and simmer for 10-15 minutes. Remove from heat.

**3.** Serve hot, garnished with chopped coriander and the remaining pomegranate seeds.

# KHASTA KACHORIS

*(Crisp, deep-fried stuffed patties)*

*Serves: 18   Preparation time: 1 hour 15 minutes   Cooking time: 1 hour*

## Ingredients

Flour *(maida)*, levelled
300 gm / 1 ½ cups
Wheat flour *(gehu ka atta)*
100 gm / ½ cup
Salt *8 gm / 1 ½ tsp*
Clarified butter *(ghee) 90 ml / 6 tbsp*
Water, chilled *105 ml / ½ cup*
Black gram, split / red gram *(dhuli urad / arhar dal)* (soaked for 3-5 hours) *100 gm / ½ cup*
Cumin *(jeera)* seeds *5 gm / 1 tsp*
Caraway seeds *(shahi jeera)*
*4 gm / ¾ tsp*
Fennel *(saunf)* seeds *8 gm / 1 ½ tsp*
Coriander *(dhaniya)* seeds
*25 gm / 1 ½ tbsp*
Black pepper *(kali mirch)*, coarsely ground *4 gm / ¾ tsp*
Water *150 ml / ⅔ cup*
Oil for frying

## Method

**1.** Blend the flours and salt in a mixing bowl. Add 4 tbsp clarified butter, rubbing it in with your fingertips until fully incorporated and the mixture resembles coarse breadcrumbs. Add chilled water and knead to form a smooth and pliable dough. Cover with plastic and set aside for half an hour.

**2. For the filling,** drain the split black gram / red gram and grind coarsely. Heat 2 tbsp clarified butter in a pan; add cumin seeds, caraway seeds, fennel seeds and coriander seeds. Fry until they splutter. Stir in black pepper, water and the coarsely ground gram. Bring to a boil, lower heat and simmer, partially covered, until the water is absorbed and the gram has softened but is still slightly firm. Cool and mix in salt to taste. Divide into 18 equal portions.

**3.** Divide the dough into 18 even portions. Shape each portion into a patty. Cover with a damp towel or plastic wrap and set aside.

**4.** Flatten each patty into a 2½" or 6.5 cm round. Place one portion of filling in the centre of the dough, then bring the sides of the dough over the filling to enclose completely. Pinch the seams together until thoroughly sealed. Cover with a plastic wrap or a moist towel. Keep aside. Shape and stuff the remaining pieces.

**5.** Heat oil in a wok *(kadhai)* till it starts smoking. Slip in a few patties (seam-side down) at a time. Fry until pale golden in colour and until they sound hollow when tapped. The crust should be delicately blistered and crisp. Drain excess oil and serve hot, accompanied by Sesame seed and tomato chutney (p. 90) and/or tomato ketchup.

### *Get-Set-Go*

*If the jelly you have set does not turn out well, add curd—about half the quantity of jelly set, sugar to taste and churn in a mixer. Set it and you will have a novel dessert.*

# IDLIS

*(Steamed rice-flour patties)*

*Serves: 4   Preparation time: 7 hours 30 minutes   Cooking time: 10-15 minutes*

## Ingredients

Parboiled rice *350 gm / 2¾ cups*
Black gram, split *(dhuli urad dal)*
*150 gm / ¾ cup*
Salt to taste
Groundnut oil *(moongphali tel)*
to grease *idli* moulds

## Method

**1.** Blend the parboiled rice to a coarse paste and soak in water for 10 minutes.
**2.** Soak split black gram in water for 1 hour and blend to make a fluffy paste.
**3.** Drain out excess water from the rice paste and mix into the gram paste along with salt. Set aside for 6 hours in a warm place.
**4.** Grease *idli* moulds with groundnut oil and pour equal quantities of the rice mixture into the moulds.
**5.** Steam in a steamer or a pressure cooker for 8-10 minutes.
**6.** Remove the *idlis* from the *idli* moulds and serve hot, accompanied by *Sambhar* (pp. 38-39) and Sesame seed and tomato chutney (p. 90).

# UTTAPAMS

*(Rice pancakes with vegetables)*

*Serves: 4    Preparation time: 1 hour 30 minutes    Cooking time: 10-15 minutes*

## Ingredients

Basmati rice *225 gm / 1 2/5 cups*
Black gram, split *(dhuli urad dal)*
*100 gm / 1½ cups*
Yoghurt *(dahi)* (p. 6) *30 gm / 2 tbsp*
Sodabicarb *5 gm / 1 tsp*
Onion, chopped *1*
Green chillies, chopped *4*
Coconut *(nariyal)*, grated *20 gm / 4 tsp*
Green coriander *(hara dhaniya)*,
chopped *20 gm / 4 tsp*
Oil *100 ml / ½ cup*

## Method

**1.** Soak rice and black gram in sufficient water for one hour.
**2.** Drain and blend the rice along with black gram. Keep aside.
**3.** Beat yoghurt and sodabicarb into the rice mixture till it becomes light and frothy.
**4.** Add onion, green chillies, coconut and green coriander and mix well. Keep aside for 20 minutes.
**5.** Heat a griddle (*tawa*) or hot plate and brush with oil. Spread a spoonful of batter evenly and cook on both sides until crisp and golden brown.
**6.** Remove, drain excess oil and serve hot, accompanied by *Sambhar* (pp. 38-39) and Sesame seed and tomato chutney (p. 90).

# SAMBHAR

*(Spicy red gram curry—a South Indian speciality)*

*Serves: 4   Preparation time: 40 minutes   Cooking time: 1 hour*

## Ingredients

Red gram *(arhar dal)* 200 gm / 1 cup
Tamarind *(imli)*, pulp 15 gm / 1 tbsp
Coconut *(nariyal)*, grated 75 gm
Coriander *(dhaniya)* seeds 5 gm / 1 tsp
Cumin *(jeera)* seeds 10 gm / 2 tsp
Red chillies, whole 2
Groundnut oil *(moongphali tel)* 45 ml / 3 tbsp
Mustard *(rai)* seeds 5 gm / 1 tsp
Asafoetida *(hing)* a pinch
Curry leaves *(meethi neem ke patte)* 15
Green chillies, slit 4
Green drumsticks *(hari saijan ki phali)*, chopped roughly 200 gm / 1 cup
Turmeric *(haldi)* powder 5 gm / 1 tsp
Red chilli powder 5 gm / 1 tsp
Onions, sliced 180 gm / 2 cups
Tomatoes, quartered 300 gm / 2½ cups
Salt to taste
Jaggery *(gur)*, soaked in 2 tbsp water 10 gm / 2 tsp
Green coriander *(hara dhaniya)*, chopped 20 gm / 4 tsp

## Method

**1.** Wash and soak red gram for 30 minutes.
**2.** Dissolve tamarind in 1 cup water.
**3.** Drain red gram and boil in a pot *(handi)* with 3 ½ cups water till completely cooked.
**4.** Prepare *sambhar* paste by lightly roasting grated coconut, coriander and cumin seeds and whole red chillies. Grind to a paste and keep aside.

**5.** Heat 2 tbsp oil, sauté mustard seeds and asafoetida till the seeds crackle. Add curry leaves, green chillies, tamarind water, green drumsticks, turmeric, red chilli powder, onions, tomatoes and salt. Bring to a boil and simmer for 7-8 minutes.

**6.** Stir in the prepared paste, the cooked red gram and the dissolved jaggery. Bring to a boil and simmer for 8-10 minutes.

**7.** Sprinkle chopped coriander and serve hot, as an accompaniment to *Idlis* (pp. 34-35) or steamed rice.

---

### *Skin(less) Onions*

*To peel sambhar onions faster, rub a little oil and turmeric powder on them and keep them in the sun for a few minutes. The skin will then come off easily.*

---

# COTTAGE CHEESE SEEKH KEBABS

*Serves: 4-5    Preparation time: 15 minutes    Cooking time: 15 minutes*

## Ingredients

Cottage cheese (*paneer*) (p. 8), finely grated *1 kg*
Garam masala (p. 6) *10 gm / 2 tsp*
Ginger (*adrak*) paste (p. 8) *25 gm / 5 tsp*
Green chillies, chopped *6*
Lemon juice *15 ml / 1 tbsp*
Onions, grated *150 gm / ¾ cup*
Red chilli powder *5 gm / 1 tsp*
Salt for seasoning
White pepper (*safed mirch*) powder *5 gm / 1 tsp*
Butter for basting *20 gm / 4 tsp*
Cornflour (*makkai ka atta*) *15 gm / 1 tbsp*

## Method

**1.** Mix all the ingredients, adding the cornflour in the end.
**2.** Divide this mixture into 15 equal balls.
**3.** Preheat the oven to 150-175 °C / 300-350 °F.
**4.** Skewer each ball. Spread by pressing along the length of the skewer with a wet hand, making each kebab about 8-10 cm long, 1 cm apart.
**5.** Roast in oven/tandoor/charcoal grill for 5-6 minutes. Baste with melted butter and roast for another 2 minutes. Remove from skewers.
**6.** Garnish with slices of cucumber, tomato, onion and serve hot, accompanied by Sesame seed and tomato chutney or Anjeer chutney (pp. 90-91).

# YAM KEBABS

*Serves: 4    Preparation time: 20 minutes    Cooking time: 20 minutes*

## Ingredients

Yam *(jimikand)* *1½ kg*
Green chillies, finely chopped
*5 gm / 1 tsp*
Ginger *(adrak)*, finely chopped
*5 gm / 1 tsp*
Salt *8 gm / 1½ tsp*
White pepper *(safed mirch)* powder
*5 gm / 1 tsp*
Red chilli powder *5 gm / 1 tsp*
Chaat masala *5 gm / 1 tsp*
Green coriander *(hara dhaniya)*,
finely chopped
*5 gm / 1 tsp*
Breadcrumbs *100 gm / ½ cup*
Oil *150 ml / ¾ cup*

## Method

**1.** Peel and wash the yam. Immerse in boiling water and cook until it becomes tender.

**2.** Remove from water, grate finely and squeeze out all the excess water.

**3.** Add the remaining ingredients to the grated yam. Mix well and divide into 8 equal portions. Shape the portions into medallions.

**4.** Shallow fry on medium heat till they become crisp and golden brown on both sides.

**5.** Serve hot, accompanied by Sesame seed and tomato chutney (p. 90).

# MATTAR KACHORIS

*(Stuffed pea patties)*

*Serves: 18   Preparation time: 1 hour 15 minutes   Cooking time: 1 hour*

## Ingredients

Flour *(maida)*, levelled *400 gm / 2 cups*
Salt *5 gm / 1 tsp*
Sugar *7 gm / 1 ½ tsp*
Clarified butter *(ghee) 75 ml / 5 tbsp*
Peas *(mattar)*, boiled, mashed
*500 gm / 2 ½ cups*
Water, chilled *105 ml / ½ cup*
Green chillies, deseeded,
finely chopped *2-3*
Ginger *(adrak)*, finely chopped
*7 gm / 1 ½ tsp*
Asafoetida *(hing)* powder *a pinch*
Garam masala (p. 6) *5 gm / 1 tsp*
Lemon juice *7 ml / 1 ½ tsp*
Baking soda *a pinch*
Oil for frying

## Method

**1.** Blend flour, salt and ½ tsp sugar in a mixing bowl. Add 4 tbsp clarified butter, rubbing it in with your fingertips until it is fully incorporated and the mixture resembles coarse breadcrumbs. Mix in 1 cup mashed peas. Add chilled water and knead to form a smooth and pliable dough. Cover with plastic wrap and set aside for half an hour.

**2. For the filling,** heat 1 tbsp clarified butter in a pan. Add green chillies and ginger and fry for half a minute. Mix in the asafoetida, 1½ cups peas, garam masala, lemon juice, baking soda and 1 tsp sugar. Stir-fry for 1 minute. Remove and allow to cool. Divide the filling into 18 portions.

**3.** Divide the dough into 18 even portions. Shape each

portion into a patty. Cover with a damp towel or plastic wrap and set aside.

**3.** Flatten each patty into a 2 ½" / 6.5 cm round. Place one portion of filling in the centre of the dough, bring the sides of the dough over the filling to enclose completely. Pinch the seams until sealed. Cover with a plastic wrap or a moist towel. Keep aside. Shape and stuff the remaining pieces.

**4.** Heat oil in a wok *(kadhai)* till it starts smoking. Slip in a few patties (seam-side down) at a time. Fry until pale golden in colour and until they sound hollow when tapped. The crust should be delicately blistered and crisp. Drain excess oil and serve hot, accompanied by Sesame seed and tomato chutney (p. 91) and / or tomato ketchup.

---

## *Lemony Tomatoes*

*When bottled tomato sauce is almost finished, add a little lime juice to it. Shake well and use it as a substitute for tomatoes in curries.*

---

# GRAM-FLOUR PANCAKES

*Serves: 4　Preparation time: 30 minutes　Cooking time: 30 minutes*

## Ingredients

Gram flour *(besan)* 150 gm / ¾ cup
Cumin *(jeera)* powder 5 gm / 1 tsp
Turmeric *(haldi)* powder 5 gm / 1 tsp
Red chilli powder *3 gm / ½ tsp*
Salt to taste
Green chillies, chopped *5 gm / 1 tsp*
Green coriander *(hara dhaniya)*, chopped *10 gm / 2 tsp*
Water as required
Cottage cheese *(paneer)* (p. 8) *100 gm / ½ cup*
Tomatoes, chopped *45 gm / 3 tbsp*
Onions, chopped *45 gm / 3 tbsp*
Oil for frying

## Method

**1.** Mix gram flour, cumin powder, turmeric powder, red chilli powder, salt, green chillies, green coriander and water to make a batter of spreading consistency.
**2.** Cut the cottage cheese into small cubes and mix with tomatoes and onions.
**3.** Heat a flat pan, brush with oil and spread batter to make a pancake of 7" diameter. Cook till crisp on both sides. Sprinkle a little oil to prevent the pancake from sticking to the pan.
**4.** Sprinkle some of the cottage cheese mixture on top and remove from heat.
**5.** Repeat the same process with the rest of the batter and cottage cheese mixture.
**6.** Serve hot.

# VEGETABLE PAPPAD ROLLS

*(Vegetable wafer rolls)*

*Serves: 4    Preparation time: 20 minutes    Cooking time: 5 minutes*

## Ingredients

Wafers *(pappad)*, medium-sized *4*
Carrot *(gajar)*, medium-sized, chopped *1*
Potato, medium-sized, chopped *1*
French beans *(fransi bean)*, chopped *6*
Cauliflower *(phool gobi)*, chopped *100 gm / ½ cup*
Tomato, chopped *1*
Turmeric *(haldi)* powder *3 gm / ½ tsp*
Red chilli powder *3 gm / ½ tsp*
Coriander *(dhaniya)* leaves, chopped *15 gm / 1 tbsp*
Salt to taste
Oil

## Method

**1.** Boil the chopped carrot, potato, French beans and cauliflower with a pinch of salt till three-fourths cooked. Drain water and dry the vegetables.

**2.** Fry the chopped tomato in 1 tbsp oil. Add boiled vegetables, fry well, add turmeric and chilli powder. Stir and then add coriander leaves. Remove from heat and cool.

**3.** Take each *pappad* and dip it in water (so that it becomes pliable). Put a little mixture along the centre and roll it like a *dosa*. Press each end well to seal.

**4.** Heat oil till it starts smoking. Deep fry the *pappad* rolls on each side till crisp. Remove and serve hot.

# BEDVI

*(Split black gram savoury rolls)*

*Serves: 4    Preparation time: 55 minutes    Cooking time: 10 minutes*

## Ingredients

Black gram, split *(dhuli urad dal)*, washed *100 gm / ½ cup*
Flour *(maida)*, sieved *100 gm / ½ cup*
Salt *7 gm / 1½ tsp*
Semolina *(suji) 200 gm / 1 cup*
Water *145 ml / ¾ cup*
Ginger *(adrak)*, chopped *15 gm / 1 tbsp*
Green chillies, chopped *10 gm / 2 tsp*
Onion seeds *(kalonji) a pinch*
Asafoetida *(hing) powder a pinch*
Garam masala *(p. 6) a pinch*
Vegetable soda *2 gm / ½ tsp*
Oil  *20 ml / 4 tsp*
Oil for frying

## Method

**1.** Pick, wash and soak the split black gram in water for 45 minutes.
**2.** Mix the flour, salt and semolina. Add water and make a medium-strong dough. Flatten the dough with wet fingertips and divide into 16 equal parts.
**3. For the filling,** grind the drained gram, ginger and green chillies to a paste. Add onion seeds, asafoetida, garam masala and vegetable soda. Divide into 16 equal parts.
**4.** Flatten one part of the dough and place one part of the filling in it. Shape into a ball.
**5.** Roll out each ball to a diameter of 5 cm, using oil.
**6.** Deep fry in hot oil till golden brown. Drain excess oil and serve hot.

# DAHI BHALLAS

*(Split black gram dumplings in tangy yoghurt)*

*Serves: 4   Preparation time: 2 hours   Cooking time: 30 minutes*

## Ingredients

**For the *bhallas*:**
Black gram, split *(dhuli urad dal)*
200 gm / 1 cup
Water *600 ml / 3 cups*
Salt *3 gm / ½ tsp*
Cumin *(jeera)* seeds *5 gm / 1 tsp*
Ginger *(adrak)*, chopped
*10 gm / 2 tsp*
Green chillies, chopped *5 gm / 1 tsp*
Oil *250 ml / 1 ¼ cups*

**For the yoghurt mixture:**
Yoghurt *(dahi)* (p. 6), thick, whisked
*400 gm / 2 cups*
Sugar *5 gm / 1 tsp*
Salt *3 gm / ½ tsp*
Cumin *(jeera)* seeds, roasted, pounded *4 gm / ¾ tsp*
Black rock salt *(kala namak) 3 gm / ½ tsp*
White pepper *(safed mirch)* powder *3 gm / ½ tsp*

**For garnishing:**
Ginger *(adrak)*, julienned (long, thin strips) *5 gm / 1 tsp*
Green chillies, julienned (long, thin strips) *5 gm / 1 tsp*
Green coriander *(hara dhaniya)*, chopped *5 gm / 1 tsp*
Red chilli powder *a pinch*
Cumin *(jeera)* seeds, roasted, pounded *a pinch*
Mint *(pudina)* leaves *4 sprigs*
Tamarind chutney *(saunth) 45 gm / 3 tbsp*

## Method

**1. For the *bhallas*,** clean the black gram and soak in water for 2 hours. Drain and grind to a fine paste, adding very little water. Remove to a mixing bowl and

add salt, cumin, ginger and green chillies. Mix well and shape into even-sized balls.

**2.** Heat oil in a *wok (kadhai)*, add the prepared balls, a few at a time, and deep fry till golden brown. (Make a hole in the centre of the ball with the thumb just before frying.) Remove and drain on paper towels.

**3.** Soak the prepared *bhallas* in lukewarm water till soft.

**4. For the yoghurt mixture,** add all the ingredients and mix well.

**5.** Remove the *bhallas* from water, squeeze out excess water and add to the yoghurt mixture. Keep aside for 10-15 minutes.

**6.** Serve chilled, garnished with ginger, green chillies, green coriander, red chilli powder, cumin powder, mint leaves and tamarind chutney.

---

### *Quick-Fix Yoghurt*

*In winter, if yoghurt takes too long to set, try this: heat a griddle (tawa) till it is really hot, then turn off the gas. Place the yoghurt vessel on the griddle and cover with a tea cosy; the yoghurt will set by the next morning.*

---

# KHANDVI

*(Savoury pancakes)*

*Serves: 4   Preparation time: 45 minutes   Cooking time: 7-10 minutes*

## Ingredients

Gram flour *(besan)*, sieved
*250 gm / 1 ¼ cups*
Yoghurt *(dahi)* (p. 6), whisked
*500 gm / 2 ½ cups*
Lemons *2*
Green chilli paste (p. 6) *5 gm / 1 tsp*
Ginger *(adrak)* paste (p. 8)
*8 gm / 1 ½ tsp*
Salt *15 gm / 1 tbsp*
Turmeric *(haldi)* powder *a pinch*
Water *500 ml / 2 ½ cups*
Oil *20 ml / 4 tsp*
Mustard *(rai)* seeds *20 gm / 4 tsp*
Cucumber *(khira)*, chopped
*70 gm / 4 ⅔ tbsp*
Capsicum *(Shimla mirch)*, chopped
*40 gm / 2 ⅔ tbsp*
Green coriander *(hara dhaniya)*, chopped *20 gm / 4 tsp*
Coconut *(nariyal)*, grated *100 gm / ½ cup*

## Method

**1.** Mix gram flour, lemon juice, green chilli paste, ginger paste, salt and turmeric to the yoghurt. Whisk well to break all lumps. Mix in water and whisk again.
**2.** Cook the mixture till it thickens, stirring continuously to prevent it from sticking to the bottom.
**3.** Oil a smooth surface, spread the mixture evenly to a thickness of 1 mm. Leave it to cool.
**4.** Heat oil, sauté mustard seeds. Add cucumber, capsicum, coriander and coconut. Toss till slightly crunchy. Sprinkle over the cooked gram-flour sheet.
**5.** Cut the sheet into 1½" strips. Roll each strip tightly. Serve hot, garnished with chopped coriander.

# SEMOLINA FRITTERS

*Serves: 4-6   Preparation time: 25 minutes   Cooking time: 10 minutes*

## Ingredients

Semolina *(suji) 150 gm / 1 ½ cups*
Yoghurt *(dahi)* (p. 6) *120 gm / 1 cup*
Water *120 ml / 1 cup*
Peas *(mattar) 100 gm / ½ cup*
Onions, small, chopped *2*
Green chillies, finely chopped *2*
Coriander *(dhaniya)* leaves, chopped *15 gm / 1 tbsp*
Salt
Asafoetida *(hing) a pinch* (optional)
Oil for frying

## Method

**1.** Sieve semolina into a large bowl. Add yoghurt and water and mix well. Set aside for 20-30 minutes.

**2.** Add peas, chopped onions, green chillies, coriander, salt, asafoetida and a little oil to the semolina mixture and mix well.

**3.** Heat oil in a wok *(kadhai)* till it starts smoking.

**4.** Divide batter into small portions and deep fry until crisp and brown. Serve hot with Sesame seed and tomato chutney (p. 90) or Anjeer chutney (p. 91).

# DHOKLA

*(Steamed savoury gram-flour dish)*

*Serves: 4   Preparation time: 45 minutes   Cooking time: 30 minutes*

## Ingredients

Gram flour *(besan)* 500 gm / 2 ½ cups
Tartar powder *12 gm / 2 tsp*
Water *400 ml / 2 cups*
Oil *45 ml / 3 tbsp*
Vegetable soda *12 gm / 2 tsp*
Cumin *(jeera)* seeds *10 gm / 2 tsp*
Green chillies, chopped *10 gm / 2 tsp*
Green coriander *(hara dhaniya)*,
chopped *45 gm / 3 tbsp*
Coconut *(nariyal)*, grated
*120 gm / ½ cup*
Lemons *2*
Ginger *(adrak)*, chopped *10 gm / 2 tsp*
Salt *20 gm / 4 tsp*
Mustard *(rai)* seeds *20 gm / 4 tsp*
Green chillies, slit *30 gm / 2 tbsp*

## Method

**1.** Dissolve tartar powder in a little water.
**2.** Sieve gram flour. Add the rest of the water to it and mix well. Add 1½ tbsp oil, tartar dissolved in water and vegetable soda. Mix well. Pour the gram-flour mixture into a flat tray; steam for 15 minutes and cool.
**3.** Blend together the cumin seeds, green chillies, green coriander, coconut, juice of two lemons, ginger and salt. Keep aside. Heat the remaining oil in a pan. Add the mustard seeds and sauté. Add the green chillies and two cups of water. Bring to a boil and pour over the steamed gram flour. Keep aside to soak.
**4.** Slice the prepared gram flour into two. Apply paste evenly on one half and place the other half back on top. Cut into square dices and serve.

# GARLIC PAPPADS

*(Garlic wafers)*

*Serves: 4   Preparation time: 24 hours*

## Ingredients

Black gram, split (*dhuli urad dal*)
Flour *200 gm / 1 cup*
Garlic *(lasan)*, chopped *30 gm / 2 tbsp*
Green chillies, chopped *10 gm / 2 tsp*
Salt to taste
Yellow chilli powder *5 gm / 1 tsp*
Oil *30 ml / 2 tbsp*
Water *250 ml / 1 ¼ cups*

## Method

**1.** Mix the split black gram flour along with garlic, green chillies, salt, yellow chilli powder and oil.

**2.** Knead to a stiff dough using water. Divide the dough into 30 even-sized balls and roll out into very thin discs.

**3.** Spread the discs on a clean sheet and allow to dry in the sun for a day or two.

**4.** Serve roasted or fried as an accompaniment to any meal.

# ALOO KACHORIS

*(Deep-fried, stuffed potato patties)*

*Serves: 18   Preparation time: 1 hour 15 minutes   Cooking time: 1 hour*

## Ingredients

Flour *(maida)*, levelled
400 gm / 2 cups
Salt *5 gm / 1 tsp*
Clarified butter *(ghee)* 60 ml / 4 tbsp
Yoghurt *(dahi)* (p. 6) *30 ml / 2 tbsp*
Water, chilled *105 ml / ½ cup*
Green chillies, deseeded, finely
chopped *2-3*
Ginger *(adrak)*, finely chopped
*7 gm / 1 ½ tsp*
Potatoes, boiled, mashed
*300 gm / 1 ½ cups*
Coriander *(dhaniya)* powder
*7 gm / 1 ½ tsp*
Cumin *(jeera)*, ground *5 gm / 1 tsp*
Fennel *(saunf)*, ground *2 gm / ½ tsp*
Garam masala (p. 6) *5 gm / 1 tsp*
Turmeric *(haldi)* powder *a pinch*
Lemon juice *15 ml / 1 tbsp*
Salt *5 gm / 1 tsp*
Green coriander *(hara dhaniya)*, finely
chopped *30 gm / 2 tbsp*
Oil for frying

## Method

**1.** Blend flour and salt in a mixing bowl. Add clarified butter, rub it in with fingertips until fully incorporated and the mixture resembles coarse breadcrumbs. Add yoghurt, 6 tbsp chilled water and knead to make a smooth and pliable dough. Cover with plastic wrap and set aside for half an hour.

**2. For the filling,** combine the remaining ingredients

in a mixing bowl and knead with hands until well blended. Divide into 18 portions; keep aside.

**3.** Divide the dough into 18 even portions. Shape each portion into a patty. Cover with a damp towel or plastic wrap and set aside.

**4.** Flatten each patty into a 2½" or 6.5 cm round. Place one portion of filling in the centre of the dough, then bring the sides of the dough over the filling to enclose completely. Pinch the seams together until thoroughly sealed. Cover with a plastic wrap or a moist towel. Keep aside. Shape and stuff the remaining patties.

**5.** Heat oil in a wok *(kadhai)* till it starts smoking. Slip in a few patties (seam-side down) at a time. Fry until pale golden in colour and until they sound hollow when tapped. The crust should be delicately blistered and crisp. Drain excess oil and serve hot, accompanied by Sesame seed and tomato chutney (p. 91) and/or tomato ketchup.

---

### *Preserving Potatoes*

*If you peel more potatoes than required, keep them in cold water to which 1 tsp of vinegar is added. They will remain fresh for 4-5 days.*

---

# LENTIL CROQUETTES

*Serves: 4    Preparation time: 30 minutes    Cooking time: 10 minutes*

## Ingredients

Lentils *(masoor dal)* 300 gm / 1½ cups
Cumin *(jeera)* seeds 5 gm / 1 tsp
Onions, chopped 60 gm / ½ cup
Ginger *(adrak)*, chopped 30 gm / 2 tbsp
Green coriander *(hara dhaniya)*
20 gm / 1 tbsp
Green chillies 5
Salt to taste
Oil for frying

## Method

**1.** Soak lentils for 6 hours. Drain and grind coarsely along with cumin seeds.
**2.** Add onions, ginger, coriander leaves, green chillies and salt. Mix well, divide into equal-sized portions and shape into round croquettes / cutlets.
**3.** Deep fry in hot oil till crisp and golden brown.
**4.** Serve hot, accompanied by chutney (pp. 90-91).

# DAL VADAS

*(Split black gram savouries)*

*Serves: 4   Preparation time: 30 minutes   Cooking time: 10 minutes*

## Ingredients

Black gram, split (*dhuli urad dal*)
300 gm / 1 ½ cups
Cumin (*jeera*) seeds 5 gm / 1 tsp
Onions, chopped 60 gm / ½ cup
Ginger (*adrak*), chopped
30 gm / 2 tbsp
Green coriander (*hara dhaniya*)
20 gm / 1 tbsp
Green chillies 5
Salt to taste
Oil for frying

## Method

**1.** Wash the split black gram in water and soak for 6 hours.
**2.** Drain gram and grind coarsely along with cumin seeds, adding very little water. Remove into a mixing bowl.
**3.** Add chopped onions, ginger, coriander leaves, green chillies and salt. Mix well with a wooden spoon.
**4.** Shape into round patties and deep fry in hot oil.
**5.** Serve with Sesame seed and tomato chutney (p. 90) or tomato sauce.

# CORN CROQUETTES

*Serves: 2-3   Preparation time: 15 minutes   Cooking time: 5-10 minutes*

## Ingredients

Corn *(makkai)*, fresh, grated
200 gm / 1 cup
Bread slices 2
Ginger *(adrak)* paste (p. 8) *5 gm / 1 tsp*
Green chilli paste (p. 6) *5 gm / 1 tsp*
White pepper *(safed mirch)* powder
*3 gm / ½ tsp*
Coriander *(dhaniya)* leaves
*15 gm / 1 tbsp*
Salt to taste

## Method

**1.** Mix all the ingredients together.
**2.** Divide the mixture into lemon-sized balls. Flatten each ball into a desired shape.
**3.** Heat oil till it starts smoking and shallow fry the croquettes till golden brown on each side.
**4.** Serve hot with Sesame seed and tomato chutney (p. 90).

# POTATO AND SAGO PATTIES

*Serves: 4   Preparation time: 30 minutes   Cooking time: 10 minutes*

## Ingredients

Potatoes (boiled) *5*
Sago (*sabu dana*) *30 gm / 2 tbsp*
Green chillies *3*
Ginger (*adrak*), chopped
*20 gm / 1 tbsp*
Green coriander (*hara dhaniya*),
chopped *15 gm / 1 tbsp*
Onion, chopped *40 gm / 2 ½ tbsp*
Curry leaves *(meethi neem
ke patte) 10*
Salt to taste
Chaat masala *5 gm / 1 tsp*
Red chilli powder *2 gm / ½ tsp*
Oil for frying

## Method

**1.** Soak sago in a cup of water for 1 hour. Drain and keep aside.

**2.** Peel and grate boiled potatoes. Add the deseeded and chopped green chillies, ginger, coriander, onion, chopped curry leaves, drained sago, salt, chaat masala and red chilli powder. Mix well with a wooden spoon.

**3.** Divide into 16 portions and shape into round patties, using a little oil on your palms.

**4.** Deep fry the patties until they are crisp and golden brown.

**5.** Serve with Sesame seed and tomato chutney (p.90) or tomato sauce.

# RASAM

*(Tamarind-flavoured soup-like dish)*

*Serves: 4   Preparation time: 30 minutes   Cooking time: 15 minutes*

## Ingredients

Red gram *(arhar dal)* 100 gm / ½ cup
Oil *15 ml / 1 tbsp*
Mustard *(rai)* seeds *5 gm / 1 tsp*
Whole red chillies *5*
Curry leaves *(meethi neem ke patte) 10*
Asafoetida *(hing) 1 gm / a pinch*
Garlic *(lasan)*, crushed *30 gm / 2 tbsp*
Turmeric *(haldi)* powder *5 gm / 1 tsp*
Tomatoes, quartered *2-3*
Peppercorns *(kali mirch)*, pounded *3-4*
Green chilli *1*
Tamarind *(imli),* pulp *100 gm / ½ cup*
Salt to taste

## Method

**1.** Heat oil in a saucepan. Add mustard seeds and sauté until they begin to crackle. Add whole red chillies, curry leaves, asafoetida and crushed garlic; stir for a few seconds.

**2.** Add turmeric, washed and cleaned red gram, tomatoes, peppercorns, slit green chilli, tamarind pulp and salt. Stir and add water.

**3.** Bring to a boil, then simmer until the *dal* is mashed.

**4.** Serve hot as a starter or as an accompaniment to a meal.

# TOMATO SHORBA

*(Tangy and spicy tomato soup)*

*Serves: 4    Preparation time: 30 minutes    Cooking time: 45 minutes*

## Ingredients

Tomatoes *800 gm*
Oil *60 ml / 4 tbsp*
Cinnamon *(dalchini) 5 gm / 1 tsp*
Cloves *(laung) 5 gm / 1 tsp*
Bayleaves *(tej patta) 2*
Green cardamoms *(choti elaichi) 4*
Ginger *(adrak)*, chopped
*15 gm / 1 tbsp*
Garlic *(lasan)*, chopped *15 gm / 1 tbsp*
Water *1 lt / 5 cups*
Salt to taste
Pepper *(kali mirch)* to taste
Cream *60 gm / 4 tbsp*

## Method

**1.** Heat oil in a deep pan; add all the whole spices and sauté till they crackle.

**2.** Add tomatoes along with ginger, garlic and water. Bring to a boil and cook on low heat for 30 minutes.

**3.** Remove from heat and mash the tomatoes. Strain the liquid through a soup strainer into another pan.

**4.** Heat the strained soup; adjust seasoning to taste and stir in cream.

**5.** Mix well and remove from heat. Serve hot.

# DAHI-PUDINA SHORBA

*(Mint-flavoured, tangy yoghurt soup)*

*Serves: 4   Preparation time: 20 minutes   Cooking time: 40 minutes*

## Ingredients

Water *500 ml / 2 ½ cups*
Yoghurt *(dahi)* (p. 6) *500 gm / 2 ½ cups*
Salt to taste
Black pepper *(kali mirch)* powder
*5 gm / 1 tsp*
Cumin *(jeera)* powder, roasted
*5 gm / 1 tsp*
Lemon juice *30 ml / 2 tbsp*
Cream *150 gm / ¾ cup*
Mint *(pudina)* leaves, chopped
*45 gm / 3 tbsp*

## Method

**1.** Heat water in a pan and slowly blend in yoghurt.
**2.** Stir in salt to taste, black pepper powder, cumin powder and lemon juice. Cook on low heat for 15 minutes.
**3.** Add cream and mint leaves; stir and cook on low heat for another 10 minutes.
**4.** Remove from heat and transfer to serving bowls. Serve hot.

# THANDAI

*(Almond milk)*

*Serves: 4    Preparation time: 5 minutes    Cooking time: 30 minutes*

## Ingredients

Milk *1 lt / 5 cups*
Saffron (*kesar*) *a few strands*
Green cardamom (*choti elaichi*) powder *10 gm / 2 tsp*
Black pepper (*kali mirch*) powder *5 gm / 1 tsp*
Almond (*badam*) powder *100 gm / ½ cup*
Melon seeds (*magaz*), powdered *45 gm / 3 tbsp*
Poppy seeds (*khus khus*), powdered *30 gm / 2 tbsp*
Sugar *100 gm / ½ cup*

## Method

**1.** Boil the milk in a pan and allow to cool. Dissolve saffron in a little milk and add to the boiled milk.
**2.** Add the green cardamom, black pepper, almond, melon seed and poppy seed powders; add sugar. Mix well and transfer to serving glasses.
**3.** Chill in a refrigerator and serve.

# SHAHI TUKDA

*(Fried bread slices in rich milk concentrate)*

*Serves: 4-5   Preparation time: 10 minutes   Cooking time: 50 minutes*

## Ingredients

White bread (double *roti*)
(cut into ¾" pieces)
*10 slices*
Clarified butter (*ghee*)
*150 gm / ¾ cup*
Milk, full cream *1 lt / 5 cups*
Sugar *300 gm / 1 ½ cups*
Pistachios (*pista*) *25 gm / 5 tsp*
Saffron (*kesar*) (dissolved in 1 tbsp
warm milk) *1 gm / ¼ tsp*
**For the sugar syrup:**
Sugar *60 gm / 4 tbsp*
Water *200 ml / 1 cup*
Rose water (*gulab jal*) *4 drops*

## Method

**1. For the sugar syrup,** add sugar to the water and boil till the water is reduced to half. Cool and add rose water.

**2.** Remove the crusts from the bread slices. Fry to a golden colour in clarified butter (*tukdas*).

**3.** Soak the slices in the cooled syrup.

**4.** Boil milk in a heavy-bottomed pot. Simmer uncovered for 30-45 minutes, until its consistency is slightly thick. Stir in sugar.

**5.** Cook for another 3-4 minutes, until the sugar is completely dissolved *(rabri)*. Cool and chill.

**6.** Pour *rabri* over fried *tukdas* on a platter. Garnish with pistachios and saffron.

# RASGOOLAS

*(Cream cheese dumplings in syrup)*

*Serves: 8   Preparation time: 2 hours   Cooking time: 50 minutes*

## Ingredients

Whole milk *2 lt / 10 cups*
Lemon juice *60 ml / 4 tbsp*
Water *2 lt / 8 cups*
Sugar *1 ½ kg*
Cornstarch (dissolved in 2 tbsp water) *15 gm / 1 tbsp*
Vetivier *(kewda)* essence *3 gm / ½ tsp*

## Method

**1.** Boil milk in a heavy-bottomed pan; reduce heat and add lemon juice to curdle milk. Remove from heat and keep aside for 10 minutes.

**2.** Pour the cheese-whey mixture into a moist cheesecloth, gather the four corners of the cloth and rinse it under tap water for about 10 minutes. Gently twist the cloth to squeeze out excess water. Tie up the corners and hang for 20 minutes to allow all excess water to drain.

**3.** Boil sugar and water in a pan until the sugar dissolves completely. Cook on high heat for 3-4 minutes; remove from heat and keep aside.

**4.** Unwrap the cheese on a clear work surface and crumble it repeatedly till it becomes fluffy and smooth.

**5.** Coat with a thin layer of oil. Divide into 16 portions and shape into smooth balls.

**6.** Reheat the sugar syrup, bring to a boil and slide in the prepared balls. Increase heat and boil continuously for about 20 minutes, adding cornstarch with ¼ cup water after 4 minutes of boiling. Add another ¼ cup of water to maintain the consistency of syrup. Take care to add the water directly into the syrup and not on the balls. Remove from heat.

**7.** Allow to cool for 10 minutes, sprinkle the vetivier essence. Leave the *rasgoolas* to soak at room temperature for at least 4 hours. Serve chilled or at room temperature along with syrup.

---

### *Badiya Barfi*

*While preparing barfi or ladoos, roast the gram flour in an oven. You will need less ghee and the taste will be far better.*

---

# BADAM HALWA

*(Almond dessert)*

*Serves: 4-5   Preparation time: 30 minutes   Cooking time: 20 minutes*

## Ingredients

Almonds (*badam*), blanched, chopped 500 gm / 2 ½ cups
Clarified butter (*ghee*) 200 gm / 1 cup
Milk 200 ml / 1 cup
Sugar 500 gm / 2 ½ cups
Green cardamom (*choti elaichi*) powder 6 gm / 1 ⅓ tsp
Saffron (*kesar*) 1 gm / ¼ tsp
Silver leaves (*varq*) (optional)

## Method

**1.** In a food processor, grind the almonds with a little milk to make a fine paste.
**2.** Heat the clarified butter in a heavy pan. Add the almond paste and cook over medium heat until the almond paste becomes light golden.
**3.** Add the milk and sugar and cook over medium heat for 10-15 minutes, until the moisture evaporates and the mixture becomes thick. Remove from heat.
**4.** Add cardamom powder and saffron.
**5.** To serve cold, spread on a greased flat tray, cut into small squares and decorate with silver leaves. To serve hot, ladle individual portions onto dessert plates and decorate with silver leaves.

# MANGO KULFI

*(Home-made mango ice cream)*

*Serves: 4-6    Preparation time: 20 minutes    Cooking time: 30 minutes + 8 hours*

## Ingredients

Mango *(aam)* pulp
*450 gm / 2 ¼ cups*
Milk *1 lt / 5 cups*
Sugar *45 gm / 3 tbsp*
Saffron *(kesar) a few strands*
Cream *(thick) 150 gm / ¾ cups*

## Method

**1.** Boil milk in a heavy-bottomed pan; lower heat and let it simmer. Add sugar and cook till the milk is reduced to a third and is thick and creamy.

**2.** Add mango pulp and saffron, cook further for 2 minutes. Cool to room temperature and mix in the cream.

**3.** Spoon the mixture into 6-8 moulds. Cover tightly with foil and freeze for at least 6 hours. Shake the mould thrice during the first hour of freezing.

**4.** Remove from refrigerator, dip the bottom of the moulds in hot water and invert onto serving dishes. Serve immediately.

# PISTA RASMALAI

*(Cream cheese covered with thickened milk)*

*Serves: 4-5   Preparation time: 45 minutes   Cooking time: 45 minutes*

## Ingredients

**For the *chenna* (cream cheese):**
Milk *2 lt / 10 cups*
Lemon juice *15 ml / 1 tbsp*
**For the *chenna* balls:**
Flour (*maida*) *20 gm / 4 tsp*
Baking powder *3-4 gm / ¾ tsp*
Water *800 ml / 4 cups*
Sugar *900 gm / 4 ½ cups*
**For the *rabri* (thickened milk):**
Milk, full cream *500 ml / 2 ½ cups*
Sugar *100 gm / ½ cup*
Pistachios (*pista*) blanched,
skinned, chopped *25 gm / 5 tsp*
Saffron (*kesar*) (dissolved in
15 ml milk) *2 gm / ¼ tsp*

## Method

**1.** For the ***chenna,*** heat the milk in a pan and bring to a slow boil. Remove from the heat and let it cool for 3-4 minutes.

**2.** Add lemon juice and stir. Wait until the milk curdles.

**3.** Carefully strain the curdled milk through a fine cheesecloth. Tie it up and let it hang for 30 minutes or until the liquid has completely drained off. The residue in the cheesecloth is called *chenna* or cream cheese.

**4.** Place the *chenna* in a bowl. Gradually break it up with your fingers and rub with your palm to a creamy texture.

**5.** Sieve flour and baking powder together; add the *chenna* and knead to a fine, soft dough.

**6.** Divide the dough into 20 equal balls and flatten slightly between your palms.

**7.** In a heavy pan, bring 4 cups of water to a slow boil. Add 900 gm of sugar and dissolve it over low heat to get a fine, clear syrup. Remove the scum from the surface.

**8.** Add the *chenna* balls to the syrup and boil on low heat till the balls double in size and rise to the surface (10 minutes).

**9.** Remove the balls with a slotted spoon and keep aside for 3-4 minutes. Drain any syrup and place on a serving dish.

**10. For the *rabri*,** reduce the milk to half its original quantity on low heat, stirring occasionally. Add the sugar, cool and refrigerate.

**11.** To serve, pour the chilled milk sauce over the *chenna* balls and cool in the refrigerator for at least 30 minutes. Sprinkle with chopped pistachios and saffron.

*Note:* Add saffron and 4-5 drops of rose water to the *pista rasmalai* and turn it into *kesari rasmalai* (saffron cream).

# RAJBHOG

*(Cardamom-stuffed cheese dumplings, dipped in sugar syrup)*

*Serves: 8    Preparation time: 30 minutes    Cooking time: 3-4 hours*

## Ingredients

**For the filling:**
Whole milk *320 ml / 1 ½ cups*
Sugar *30 gm / 2 tbsp*
Pistachios *(pista)*, grated *45 gm / 3 tbsp*
Green cardamoms *(choti elaichi)*, crushed *5*

**For the dumplings:**
Whole milk *2 lt / 10 cups*
Lemon juice, strained *60 ml / 4 tbsp*
Water *2 lt / 10 cups*
Sugar *1 ½ kg / 7 ½ cups*
Cornstarch (dissolved in 2 tbsp water) *15 gm / 1 tbsp*
Rose essence *½ tsp*

## Method

**1. For the filling**, boil milk and sugar in a pan till the milk reduces to half. Add the pistachios and cardamoms, cook until the mixture leaves the sides of the pan. Keep aside to cool.

**2. For the dumplings,** heat milk over high heat and bring to a boil. Reduce heat and add lemon juice to curdle the milk. Remove and keep aside.

**3.** Pour the cheese-whey mixture into a moist cheesecloth. Gather the corners of the cloth and rinse under tap water. Squeeze out excess water by gently twisting the cloth.

**4.** Boil sugar and water in a pan until sugar completely dissolves. Remove from heat and keep aside.

**5.** Unwrap the cheese on a clean work surface and crumble it. Divide into 8 balls and flatten. Divide the filling equally and place one in the centre of each patty. Roll into balls.

**6.** Heat sugar syrup and slide in the prepared balls. Boil for 20 minutes, adding cornstarch mixed in ¼ cup of water to thicken the consistency of the syrup.

**7.** Remove and allow to cool. Sprinkle rose essence and serve chilled or at room temperature.

---

### *Pop and Thicken*

*If you wish to thicken milk and are in a hurry, add some poppy seeds and watch the results!*

---

# GAJRELA

*(Rich carrot dessert)*

*Serves: 4-5   Preparation time: 10 minutes   Cooking time: 1 hour*

## Ingredients

Carrots (*gajar*), finely grated *1 kg*
Milk, full cream *1 lt / 5 cups*
Green cardamoms (*choti elaichi*) *10*
Sugar *180 gm / 1 ¾ cups*
Clarified butter (*ghee*) *60 ml / 4 tbsp*
Almonds (*badam*) *100 gm / ½ cup*
Pistachios (*pista*) *50 gm / ¼ cup*

## Method

**1.** Heat milk in a heavy pan; bring to a slow boil, stirring with a wooden spoon.
**2.** Add the grated carrots and green cardamoms and cook over medium heat for 30-45 minutes or until the milk has almost evaporated.
**3.** Add the sugar, stir and cook until it dissolves completely.
**4.** Add the clarified butter, stir and cook until the carrots are slightly caramelized.
**5.** Reduce the heat, add the almonds and pistachios, and cook for 3-4 minutes.
Serve hot, garnished with pistachio / almond flakes and grated *khoya* (p. 8).

# BESAN LADOO

*(Sweet gram-flour balls, with coconut and walnuts)*

*Makes: 2 dozen balls    Preparation time: 10 minutes    Cooking time: 20 minutes*

## Ingredients

Gram flour *(besan)*, sifted
*200 gm / 1 cup*
Butter (unsalted) / oil *180 ml / ¾ cup*
Coconut *(nariyal)*, dried, grated
*30 gm / 2 tbsp*
Walnuts *(akhrot)*, chopped
*30 gm / 2 tbsp*
Nutmeg *(jaiphal)*, ground *a pinch*
Sugar *110 gm / ½ cup*

## Method

**1.** Melt butter/oil in a heavy-bottomed pan over moderate heat. Add gram flour, coconut, walnuts and nutmeg. Cook for about 5 minutes stirring constantly. Add sugar and continue to cook for 10-15 minutes or until the mixture is thick and deep golden brown.
**2.** Transfer to a clean, flat surface. When cool enough to handle, shape into 24 equal-sized balls.
**3.** Garnish with slivered nuts and serve. (You can store these for 10-15 days.)

# GULAB JAMUNS

*(Cottage cheese dumplings in sugar syrup)*

*Serves: 4-5   Preparation time: 20 minutes   Cooking time: 2 hours 30 minutes*

## Ingredients

Cottage cheese (*paneer*) (p. 8) 70 gm / 4 1/3 tbsp
*Khoya* (p. 8) *500 gm / 2 1/2 cups*
Flour *(maida) 60 gm / 4 tbsp*
Baking soda *3 gm / 2/3 tsp*
Water *500 ml / 2 1/2 cups*
Sugar *1 kg / 5 cups*
Pistachios (*pista*), blanched, chopped *25 gm / 5 tsp*
Saffron (*kesar*) (dissolved in 15 ml milk) *1 gm / 1/4 tsp*
Green cardamom (*choti elaichi*) powder *2 gm / 1/2 tsp*
Oil for frying *500 ml / 2 1/2 cups*

## Method

**1.** Break up the *khoya* in a bowl. Add the cottage cheese and rub the mixture to a fine, creamy texture.
**2.** Sieve the flour and baking soda together; mix with the *khoya* mixture and knead to a soft dough.
**3.** Divide the dough into 20 equal-sized balls and cover with a moist cloth.
**4.** In a pan, boil together the water and sugar, removing the scum from time to time. Cook on low heat until the syrup has a one-thread consistency.
**5.** Mix the chopped pistachios, saffron dissolved in milk and cardamom powder to a thick paste. Divide the paste into 20 portions.

**6.** Insert one portion into each of the cottage cheese dumplings. Seal and make balls.
**7.** Heat the oil in a pan. Fry the dumplings over very slow heat, till they are golden in colour. Remove with a slotted spoon and transfer into the sugar syrup. Leave in the syrup for at least 1-2 hours. Serve hot with the syrup.

---

### *Bigger and Better*

*While making gulab jamuns, put a cashewnut in each one while shaping them. The gulab jamuns will look bigger and taste better.*

---

# KESAR SANDESH

*(Saffron-cheese fudge)*

*Serves: 4   Preparation time: 1 hour 30 minutes   Cooking time: 1 hour*

## Ingredients

Saffron *(kesar) 3 gm / ½ tsp*
Whole milk *320 ml / 1½ cups*
Lemon juice *60 ml / 4 tbsp*
Sugar, powdered *110 gm / ½ cup*

## Method

**1.** Roast saffron in a dry pan and pound to a fine powder. Dissolve in 2 tbsp hot milk and keep aside.
**2.** Heat milk in a pan over high heat; bring to a frothing boil, stirring continuously. Reduce heat, add lemon juice to curdle the milk and separate the cheese from the whey. If it does not, then add 1 more tbsp of lemon juice. Remove from heat and set aside to cool.
**3.** Pour the cheese-whey mixture into a moist cheesecloth. Gather the 4 corners of the cloth and rinse under tap water for 10 minutes. Gently twist the cloth to squeeze out excess water. Tie up the corners and hang for 20-30 minutes to allow all excess water to drain.

**4.** Unwrap the cheese on a clean work surface and crumble till it becomes fluffy and even. Blend in the powdered sugar and knead till it becomes smooth and grainless.

**5.** Transfer the cheese-sugar (*chenna*) mixture to a heavy-bottomed pan. Cook for 10-15 minutes until the mixture becomes a little thick and glossy.

**6.** Divide the mixture into two portions. Mix in the dissolved saffron into one portion till it turns yellow. Divide the yellow *chenna* mixture into 2 portions again.

**7.** Spread three alternate layers of yellow, white and yellow *chenna* on a buttered tray to form a 1½"- 2" thick cake. Allow to cool and cut into 1½" thick squares. Arrange on a platter and serve.

---

## *Nourishing Nutrient*

*Keep milk away from sunlight to prevent any loss in its Vitamin B content.*

---

# PHIRNI

*(Cardamom-flavoured milk pudding)*

*Serves: 4-5    Preparation time: 10 minutes    Cooking time: 30 minutes*

## Ingredients

Milk, full cream *1 lt / 5 cups*
Rice flour (*chawal ka atta*)
*100 gm / ½ cup*
Sugar *200 gm / 1 cup*
Salt a *pinch*
Green cardamom (*choti elaichi*)
powder *3 gm / ⅔ tsp* / rose water
(*gulab jal*) *4-5 drops*
Pistachios (*pista*) *50 gm / ¼ cup*
Saffron (*kesar*) (dissolved in 15 ml
milk) *1 gm / ¼ tsp*

## Method

**1.** In a heavy pan, heat half the milk and bring to a slow boil.

**2.** Dissolve the rice flour in the remaining cold milk and slowly add to the hot milk. Continue to cook over very low heat, stirring constantly, until the mixture becomes a thick, light custard.

**3.** Add sugar and a pinch of salt and cook for 2-3 minutes more until the sugar is completely dissolved.

**4.** Cool, add cardamom powder / rose water and mix well.

**5.** Serve in bowls, garnished with chopped pistachios and saffron.

# PISTA KULFI

*(Ice-cream flavoured with pistachios)*

*Serves: 4-5    Preparation time: 10 minutes    Cooking time: 3 hours*

## Ingredients

Milk, full cream *4 lt / 20 cups*
Sugar *400 gm / 2 cups*
Pistachios *(pista)*, chopped
*100 gm / ½ cup*
Green cardamom (*choti elaichi*)
powder *3 gm / ⅔ tsp*
Cherries *(gilas)*, chopped *10*

## Method

**1.** Boil milk over medium heat till it reduces to half (30-45 minutes). The consistency should be slightly thick and the colour, a pale yellow.

**2.** Gradually add the sugar, stir and cook for another 3-4 minutes until the sugar is completely dissolved.

**3.** Cool and add the chopped pistachios, cardamom powder and cherries.

**4.** Fill the mixture into small, conical-shaped aluminium containers or any even-sized container. Seal the tops with silver foil and freeze for 1½-2 hours.

**5.** Remove from moulds and serve chilled with *falooda* (cold vermicelli) (p. 89).

# FALOODA

*(Fresh cornflour vermicelli served with kulfi)*

*Serves: 4   Preparation time: 10 minutes   Cooking time: 15-20 minutes*

## Ingredients

Water *400 ml / 2 cups*
Cornflour *(makkai ka atta)*
*100 gm / ½ cup*
Yellow colour (optional) *a pinch*

## Method

**1.** Mix water and cornflour in a wok *(kadhai)* and stir thoroughly. Add the yellow colour.

**2.** Cook on low heat, stirring continuously, till the mixture thickens and becomes gelatinous. Remove from heat.

**3.** Pour into a *falooda* press and place over a container of cold water.

**4.** Press the mixture out into a platter in one continous stream without stopping.

**5.** Store the *falooda* in the refrigerator and serve chilled, as an accompaniment to *kulfi*.

**6.** If desired, you can flavour the *falooda* with Roohafza / vetivier / rose water.

# SESAME SEED AND TOMATO CHUTNEY

*Serves: 4   Preparation time: 15 minutes   Cooking time: 20 minutes*

## Ingredients

Tomatoes, chopped *200 gm / 1 cup*
Sesame (*til*) seeds *30 gm / 2 tbsp*
Groundnut oil *(moongphali tel)*
*30 ml / 2 tbsp*
Onions, chopped *150 gm / ¾ cup*
Red chilli powder *3 gm / ½ tsp*
Turmeric (*haldi*) powder
*3 gm / ½ tsp*
Asafoetida (*hing*) powder *a pinch*
Black gram (*chana dal*), roasted
*20 gm / 4 tsp*
**For the tempering:**
Oil *30 ml / 2 tbsp*
Red chillies, whole *5*
Curry leaves *(meethi neem ke patte)*
*10 gm / 2 tsp*
Mustard (*rai*) seeds *3 gm / ½ tsp*

## Method

**1.** Heat groundnut oil in a pan. Add onions and sauté till light brown.

**2.** Stir in red chilli powder, turmeric powder, asafoetida powder and sesame seeds. Stir-fry for a few minutes.

**3.** Add tomatoes along with black gram and cook further for 10 minutes.

**4.** Remove from heat and allow to cool. Blend to make a paste and remove to a bowl.

**5. For the tempering**, heat oil in a pan and add red chillies, curry leaves and mustard seeds. Sauté till they crackle and remove from heat.

**6.** Add the prepared tempering to the chutney and serve.

# ANJEER KI CHUTNEY

*(Fig chutney)*

*Serves: 4    Preparation time: 30 minutes    Cooking time: 30 minutes*

## Ingredients

Figs *(anjeer)*, dried 500 gm / 2 ½ cups
Almonds *(badam)* 60 gm / ¼ cup
Oil *100 ml / ½ cup*
Onions, chopped *100 gm / ½ cup*
Garlic *(lasan)*, chopped
*100 gm / ½ cup*
Sugar *60 gm / 4 tbsp*
Red chilli powder *5 gm / 1 tsp*
Green chillies, chopped *15 gm / 1 tbsp*
Salt to taste
Malt vinegar *(sirka) 60 ml / 4 tbsp*
White vinegar *(sirka) 25 ml / 5 tsp*
Green cardamom (*choti elaichi*)
powder *10 gm / 2 tsp*
Melon (*magaz*) seeds *10 gm / 2 tsp*

## Method

**1.** Blanch the figs and almonds in water for 10 minutes and keep aside. Fry the onions and garlic in oil until golden brown. Remove and drain.

**2.** Blend all the ingredients except green cardamom powder and melon seeds to make a paste.

**3.** Transfer to a bowl and garnish with green cardamom powder and melon seeds.

**4.** Refrigerate and use as required (can be stored in an airtight container in a refrigerator for 1-2 months).

# Glossary of Cooking Terms

**Batter :** A fluid mixture of flour, egg and milk/water used in cooking and for cooking food before frying.

**Blend :** Mix thoroughly.

**Croquettes :** Fried mixtures of meat, fish, poultry or potatoes bound together in various shapes.

**Fillet :** The undercut of a loin or ribs of meat, boned sides of fish or boned breasts of poultry.

**Fritters :** Pieces of meat, fruit or vegetables coated in batter and deep fried.

**Parboil :** Boil for part of the normal cooking time.

**Purée :** Fruit, meat, fish, vegetables pounded, sieved or pulverised in an electric blender.

**Sauté :** Fry quickly over strong heat in fat or oil.

**Soup :** A savoury liquid dish made by boiling meat, fish or vegetables, etc. in stock or water.

**Stock :** Liquid made by stewing bones, vegetables, etc. as a basis for soup, gravy or sauce.

**Whisk :** To beat air rapidly into a mixture with an egg beater, rotary beater or electric beater.

# INDEX

**SAVOURIES**
**Non-Vegetarian**

| | |
|---|---|
| Barbecued Lamb Cubes | 14 |
| Chicken-Cheese Savoury | 22 |
| Ginger Lamb Chops | 12 |
| Gosht Achari Chaap | 18 |
| Jhinga Nisha | 10 |
| Maans ke Sooley | 20 |
| Shola Kebabs | 25 |
| Tandoori Bateyr | 16 |
| Tandoori Chaat | 24 |

**Vegetarian**

| | |
|---|---|
| Aloo Kachoris | 56 |
| Bedvi | 47 |
| Chutneyed Potatoes | 26 |
| Corn Croquettes | 60 |
| Cottage Cheese Seekh Kebabs | 40 |
| Cottage Cheese Tikkas | 28 |
| Dahi Bhallas | 48 |

| | |
|---|---|
| Dal Vadas | 59 |
| Dhokla | 53 |
| Garlic Pappads | 54 |
| Gram-Flour Pancakes | 45 |
| Idlis | 34 |
| Khandvi | 51 |
| Khasta Kachoris | 32 |
| Lentil Croquettes | 58 |
| Mattar Kachoris | 42 |
| Pomegranate Potatoes | 30 |
| Potato and Sago Patties | 61 |
| Sambhar | 38 |
| Semolina Fritters | 52 |
| Uttapams | 36 |
| Vegetable Pappad Rolls | 46 |
| Yam Kebabs | 41 |

**SOUPS / STARTERS**

| | |
|---|---|
| Dahi-Pudina Shorba | 65 |
| Rasam | 62 |
| Thandai | 66 |
| Tomato Shorba | 64 |

**DESSERTS**

| | |
|---|---|
| Badam Halwa | 71 |

| | |
|---|---|
| Besan Ladoo | 80 |
| Falooda | 89 |
| Gajrela | 79 |
| Gulab Jamuns | 82 |
| Kesar Sandesh | 84 |
| Mango Kulfi | 72 |
| Phirni | 87 |
| Pista Kulfi | 88 |
| Pista Rasmalai | 74 |
| Rajbhog | 76 |
| Rasgoolas | 68 |
| Shahi Tukda | 67 |

**CHUTNEYS**

| | |
|---|---|
| Sesame Seed and Tomato Chutney | 90 |
| Anjeer ki Chutney | 91 |

# ACKNOWLEDGEMENTS

Grateful thanks to the Master Chefs at **The Intercontinental Hotel,** New Delhi, and the **Oberoi Group of Hotels,** New Delhi, for making available their kitchens for the preparation and photography of the dishes.

All rights reserved. No part of this publication may be transmitted or reproduced in any form or by any means without prior permission of the publisher.

ISBN: 978-81-7436-075-5

**© This edition Roli & Janssen BV 2011**
Fifth impression
Published in India by Roli Books in arrangement with Roli & Janssen BV
M 75, Greater Kailash II Market, New Delhi-110 048, INDIA
Tel.: ++91-11-4068 2000, Fax: ++91-11-2921 7185
E-mail: info@rolibooks.com; Website: www.rolibooks.com

Photographs: Dheeraj Paul

Printed and bound in Singapore